Level 2

The Nature Kid's Guide to STINGRAYS

DAVID ANDERSON

LP Media Inc. Publishing

For information address LP Media Inc. Publishing,
30012 Variolite St NW, Princeton MN 55371
www.lpmedia.org

Publication Data

Stingrays
The Nature Kid's Guide to Stingrays — First edition.

Summary: "Learn all about Stingrays, the Nature Kid Way"
— Provided by publisher.

ISBN: 979-8-89818-227-4

[1. Stingrays – Non-Fiction] I. Title.

Title: The Nature Kid's Guide to Stingrays

CONTENTS

Sandy Seas 4
Ray Range 6
Flat Flyers 8
Wing Shape 10
Super Sensors 12
Tail Sting 14
Crunchy Clams 16
Dig Deep 18
Shark Snacks 20
Hide Fast 22
Glide On 24
Ray Days 26
Fever Friends 28
Finding Mates 30
Tiny Pups 32
Solo Start 34
Big Threats 36
Safe Seas 38

SANDY SEAS

DID YOU KNOW?

Stingrays have been swimming in Earth's oceans for over 150 million years — since the time of the dinosaurs!

Swoosh! A stingray glides over the warm, sandy sea floor.

Slide your hand across a stingray's back and it feels like wet velvet. These remarkable animals look like they were designed by someone who flattened a shark and gave it wings.

Stingrays are not fish that happen to be flat. They are built for the seafloor. Their entire body is shaped to sink into sand, disappear from view, and wait. Two eyes on top. Mouth and gills on the bottom. Everything exactly where it needs to be.

Warm shallow coastal waters around the world are home to more than 200 species. This book is going to introduce you to some of the most incredible ones.

RAY RANGE

Splash! An ocellate river stingray darts through muddy water.

Stingrays live all around the world. Most swim in warm ocean water near the coast. You can find them near every **continent** except Antarctica.

The water near the poles is simply too cold for them. But stingrays fill warm seas everywhere else — near Asia, Africa, Australia, and the Americas.

Some rays even live in rivers! The ocellate river stingray calls South American rivers home. It never needs the salty sea at all.

Australia has more types of stingrays than any other country — over 80 different kinds!

FLAT FLYERS

FUN FACT!

A manta ray can weigh 3,000 pounds — as much as a small car!

Whoosh! A giant manta ray soars over a coral reef.

Stingrays come in many different sizes. The smallest ones are no bigger than your hand. The biggest one on Earth could stretch across your entire classroom.

That giant is the oceanic manta ray. Its wings can reach 23 feet from tip to tip — wider than a school bus is long!

Most stingrays are much smaller than that. The kind you might spot near a beach is usually about the size of a large pizza. Same shape too, if you think about it!

WING SHAPE

DID YOU KNOW?

A stingray's skin feels bumpy and rough, just like sandpaper!

Flap! A spotted eagle ray beats its long, pointed wings.

A stingray's body is flat and wide. The sides of its body are big fins that look just like wings on a bird.

Stingrays do not have any bones at all. Their whole body is made of **cartilage** — the bendy stuff in your ears and nose. This makes them flexible and light.

Spotted eagle rays have long, pointed fins and a very thin tail. White spots cover their dark blue backs like stars in a night sky.

SUPER SENSORS

FUN FACT! A stingray's nostrils are on the bottom of its head, right next to its mouth!

Zap! A stingray feels a tiny jolt of electricity. It's hunting!

Stingrays have amazing senses. Small pores on their snout can feel electricity. Every living thing gives off tiny electric signals, and stingrays detect them all.

A stingray uses this power to find prey in total darkness. Even a worm buried deep in mud gives off a signal. The ray feels it and swims right over for a meal.

Round ribbontail rays can also feel waves moving through the water. Every fish that swims nearby pushes the water and makes tiny ripples. The ray feels those ripples through its body and knows exactly where to look.

TAIL STING

A stingray can grow a brand new barb if its old one breaks off — like a lizard regrowing its tail!

Whip! A stingray snaps its sharp tail at a threat.

Most stingrays have a sharp **barb** on their tail. This barb holds venom that causes a painful sting. It is their main defense against predators.

Stingrays do not want to sting you. They only sting when scared or stepped on by accident. The sting is not meant to attack — it is meant to escape. One quick jab is usually enough to send any predator swimming the other way.

Some stingrays have one barb. Others have two or even three, giving them extra protection when danger gets too close.

CRUNCHY CLAMS

DID YOU KNOW?

Manta rays are different — they eat only tiny **plankton**, filtering thousands of gallons of water each day!

Crunch! A stingray crushes a clam shell with its jaws.

Stingrays eat many kinds of small sea creatures. Clams, shrimp, and crabs are some of their favorites. They also munch on worms and small fish.

A stingray's mouth is on the bottom of its body. Instead of sharp teeth, it has strong, flat plates. These plates crush hard shells with ease.

Southern stingrays love to eat clams and crabs. They munch and crunch all day long. A big meal can keep a ray full for many hours.

DIG DEEP

FUN FACT!

A stingray can suck food up from the sand like a vacuum cleaner!

Puff! A stingray blasts sand away to find its food.

Stingrays are clever hunters. They press their body flat on the sand, then flap their fins hard. This blows the sand away like a leaf blower.

This move digs up clams and worms hiding below. The ray drops down and grabs the food with its mouth. Dinner is served!

What makes this hunting trick even smarter is that stingrays rarely hunt alone. Small fish like wrasses and jacks follow rays around waiting for scraps. The ray stirs up the sand and everyone nearby gets a meal.

SHARK SNACKS

DID YOU KNOW?

Hammerhead sharks use their wide heads to pin stingrays flat against the sea floor!

Whoosh! A shark glides above the ocean floor looking for dinner.

Stingrays have some powerful enemies. Sharks are their biggest threat. Great hammerheads are specialized stingray hunters, and scientists have found dozens of stingray barbs embedded in the jaws and faces of hammerheads — proof of just how often these two animals tangle.

Large fish, orcas, and sea lions also hunt stingrays. Even some seabirds grab small rays in shallow water near shore.

A stingray's best defense is simply not being seen in the first place.

HIDE FAST

FUN FACT!

A stingray buried in sand can hold perfectly still for hours, barely breathing!

Zoom! A stingray sees a predator and zips toward a coral reef.

Stingrays have many ways to stay safe. Their colors match the sandy sea floor perfectly. This makes them very hard to spot.

When danger comes near, a stingray swims away fast. A quick burst of speed helps it escape. Some rays kick up clouds of sand to confuse hunters while they flee.

Blue-spotted ribbontail rays hide under coral ledges. They squeeze into tight spaces where big fish cannot fit. Staying hidden is their best trick of all.

GLIDE ON
DID YOU KNOW
Spotted eagle rays sometimes leap high above the water and belly flop back in with a big splash!

Swish! A spotted eagle ray glides like a bird in the sea.

Stingrays move by flapping their wide fins. It looks like they are flying through the water! Their smooth glide is beautiful to watch.

Some rays swim slowly along the bottom. Others soar high above the reef. The way a ray moves depends on its body shape.

Spotted eagle rays are fast, strong swimmers. They flap their pointed fins like bird wings and can race through open water at 20 miles per hour. That is faster than most people can run!

RAY DAYS

DID YOU KNOW?

Stingrays sometimes rest stacked on top of each other like pancakes — up to a dozen rays in one pile!

Shhh! A stingray settles into the sand for a long rest.

A stingray's day follows a quiet and simple rhythm. When the sun is high, most rays sink into the sand and rest. Their bodies slow down, their breathing barely visible, their flat shape hidden completely beneath the seafloor.

When darkness falls, everything changes. The ray lifts off the sand and begins to cruise. Its senses switch on, scanning the seafloor for the electric signals of buried prey.

By dawn it is back in the sand, perfectly still again, waiting for the next night to begin. Day after day, the same pattern repeats.

FEVER FRIENDS

FUN FACT!

Some fevers of stingrays can have hundreds of rays all in one place!

Swoop! Dozens of manta rays glide past like a slow parade.

A group of stingrays is called a **fever**. Some rays like to hang out together. Others prefer to be alone.

Rays in a fever may rest near each other. They do not talk or share food, but being in a group helps keep them safe. More eyes mean more chances to spot danger.

Manta rays often swim together in small groups. They meet at spots where tiny food fills the water. Sharing a good meal brings them close.

FINDING MATES

FUN FACT!

Female stingrays are almost always bigger than males — sometimes twice as heavy!

Chase! A male stingray follows after a female.

When it is time to mate, male rays follow females. The male holds on to the female's fin gently, and they swim together as a pair.

Mating often happens in warm months. Stingrays can sense when another ray is nearby. Special scents in the water lead them together from far away.

Round ribbontail rays mate in shallow water. The male swims under the female during mating. After that, they each go their own way.

TINY PUPS

DID YOU KNOW?

Some stingray pups are so small they could fit in the palm of your hand!

Cute! A baby stingray pup swims off on its own for the first time.

Baby stingrays are called pups. Most stingrays give birth to live pups instead of laying eggs. The babies grow inside their mother until they are ready.

Pups are born ready to swim and find food. They look like tiny copies of their parents! Most litters have two to six pups at a time.

Ocellate river stingray pups are born in fresh water. They have the same round spots as their parents. Even as babies, they have a small barb on their tail for protection.

SOLO START

DID YOU KNOW?

A newborn manta ray pup is already about four feet wide — bigger than most adult stingrays!

Flick! A tiny pup swims away from its mother for good.

Stingray parents do not raise their young. Once a pup is born, it is completely on its own. No lessons, no hugs, no help from mom or dad.

This may sound scary, but pups are ready. They know how to swim, hide, and find food right away. They are born knowing exactly what to do.

Manta ray mothers have just one pup at a time. The pup is already big and strong at birth. It swims away and starts its life alone in the wide ocean.

BIG THREATS

DID YOU KNOW?

Warming oceans are pushing stingrays to move to new places they have never lived before.

Snap! A fishing net tangles around a stingray's wings.

Many stingrays face big dangers today. Fishing nets catch rays by accident. When rays get trapped, they can get hurt or die.

Pollution is another serious problem. Dirty water can make stingrays sick. Plastic trash in the ocean can also harm them when they mistake it for food.

Manta rays are hunted in some parts of the world. People catch them for their body parts. This puts many manta rays in danger of disappearing forever.

SAFE SEAS

FUN FACT!

Some aquariums let visitors gently touch stingrays to help people learn to love and protect them!

Plop! A stingray slips into the calm water of a safe bay.

People around the world are working to protect stingrays. Some countries have made rules that stop people from hunting rays. Others have created protected ocean parks where fishing is not allowed, giving rays safe places to live and grow.

Scientists track rays using small tags to learn where they travel and what they need to survive. Every new discovery helps build a better plan.

You can help too. Keep beaches clean, never touch wild rays, and share what you now know about these amazing animals.

GLOSSARY

barb

A sharp spike on a stingray's tail

cartilage

Bendy body material, like the stuff in your nose and ears

continent

One of the seven big land areas on Earth

fever

A group of stingrays

plankton

Tiny living things that float in the water

www.ingramcontent.com/pod-product-compliance
Lightning Source LLC
LaVergne TN
LVHW071209160826
845679LV00003B/781

* 9 7 9 8 8 9 8 1 8 2 2 7 4 *